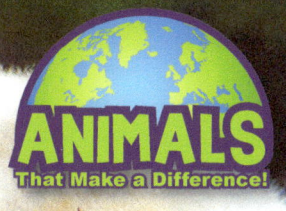

ANIMALS That Make a Difference!

Spirit Bears

Kit Caudron-Robinson

 Explore other books at:
WWW.ENGAGEBOOKS.COM

VANCOUVER, B.C.

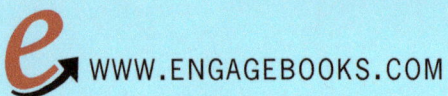
WWW.ENGAGEBOOKS.COM

Spirit Bears: Level 3
Animals That Make a Difference!
Caudron-Robinson, Kit, 1996
Text © 2024 Engage Books
Design © 2024 Engage Books

Edited by: A.R. Roumanis, Melody Sun, and Ashley Lee
Design by: Mandy Christiansen

Text set in Arial Regular.
Chapter headings set in Nathaniel-19.

FIRST EDITION / FIRST PRINTING

All rights reserved. No part of this book may be stored in a retrieval system, reproduced or transmitted in any form or by any other means without written permission from the publisher or a licence from the Canadian Copyright Licensing Agency. Critics and reviewers may quote brief passages in connection with a review or critical article in any media.

Every reasonable effort has been made to contact the copyright holders of all material reproduced in this book.

LIBRARY AND ARCHIVES CANADA CATALOGUING IN PUBLICATION

Title: Spirit bears / Kit Caudron-Robinson.
Names: Caudron-Robinson, Kit, author.
Description: Series statement: Animals that make a difference

Identifiers: Canadiana (print) 20230448577 | Canadiana (ebook) 20230448585
ISBN 978-1-77476-824-2 (hardcover)
ISBN 978-1-77476-825-9 (softcover)
ISBN 978-1-77476-826-6 (epub)
ISBN 978-1-77476-827-3 (pdf)
ISBN 978-1-77878-139-1 (audio)

Subjects:
LCSH: Kermode bear—Juvenile literature.
LCSH: Human-animal relationships—Juvenile literature.

Classification: LCC QL737.C27 C38 2024 | DDC J599.78/5—DC23

This project has been made possible in part by the Government of Canada.

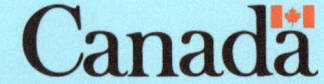

Contents

- 4 What Are Spirit Bears?
- 6 A Closer Look
- 8 Where Do Spirit Bears Live?
- 10 What Do Spirit Bears Eat?
- 12 How Do Spirit Bears Talk to Each Other?
- 14 Spirit Bear Life Cycle
- 16 Curious Facts About Spirit Bears
- 18 Where Did Spirit Bears Come From?
- 20 How Spirit Bears Help Earth
- 22 How Spirit Bears Help Other Animals
- 24 How Spirit Bears Help Humans
- 26 Spirit Bears in Danger
- 28 How to Help Spirit Bears
- 30 Quiz

What Are Spirit Bears?

Spirit bears are a type of American black bear that often have white or creamy fur. They are also called Kermode bears. To make white babies, both parents must carry **genes** that create a white coat.

KEY WORD

Genes: traits that are passed down from one family member to another.

Local **Indigenous** people kept spirit bears a secret for many years. They did this to protect them from hunters. Spirit bears are no longer a secret, but Indigenous people still protect them.

KEY WORD

Indigenous: the first people to live in a place.

A Closer Look

Spirit bears weigh between 150 and 300 pounds (68 and 136 kilograms) fully grown. They stand 3 feet (1 meter) tall. They are 4 to 6 feet (1.2 to 1.8 meters) long.

A spirit bear's long, curved claws are very strong. They help spirit bears climb trees.

Local **Indigenous** people kept spirit bears a secret for many years. They did this to protect them from hunters. Spirit bears are no longer a secret, but Indigenous people still protect them.

KEY WORD

Indigenous: the first people to live in a place.

A Closer Look

Spirit bears weigh between 150 and 300 pounds (68 and 136 kilograms) fully grown. They stand 3 feet (1 meter) tall. They are 4 to 6 feet (1.2 to 1.8 meters) long.

A spirit bear's long, curved claws are very strong. They help spirit bears climb trees.

Spirit bears have brown eyes and can see in the dark.

Spirit bears have dark brown noses. Their sense of smell is 1000 times better than a human's.

Where Do Spirit Bears Live?

Spirit bears sleep in dens, caves, or hollowed-out trees. They spend the winters **hibernating** in their dens. In the springtime, spirit bears come out to look for food again.

KEY WORD

Hibernating: Passing the winter in a sleep-like state.

Most spirit bears live in the Great Bear Rainforest in British Columbia, Canada. They are mostly found on Princess Royal Island and Gribbell Island. There are not many spirit bears outside of this area.

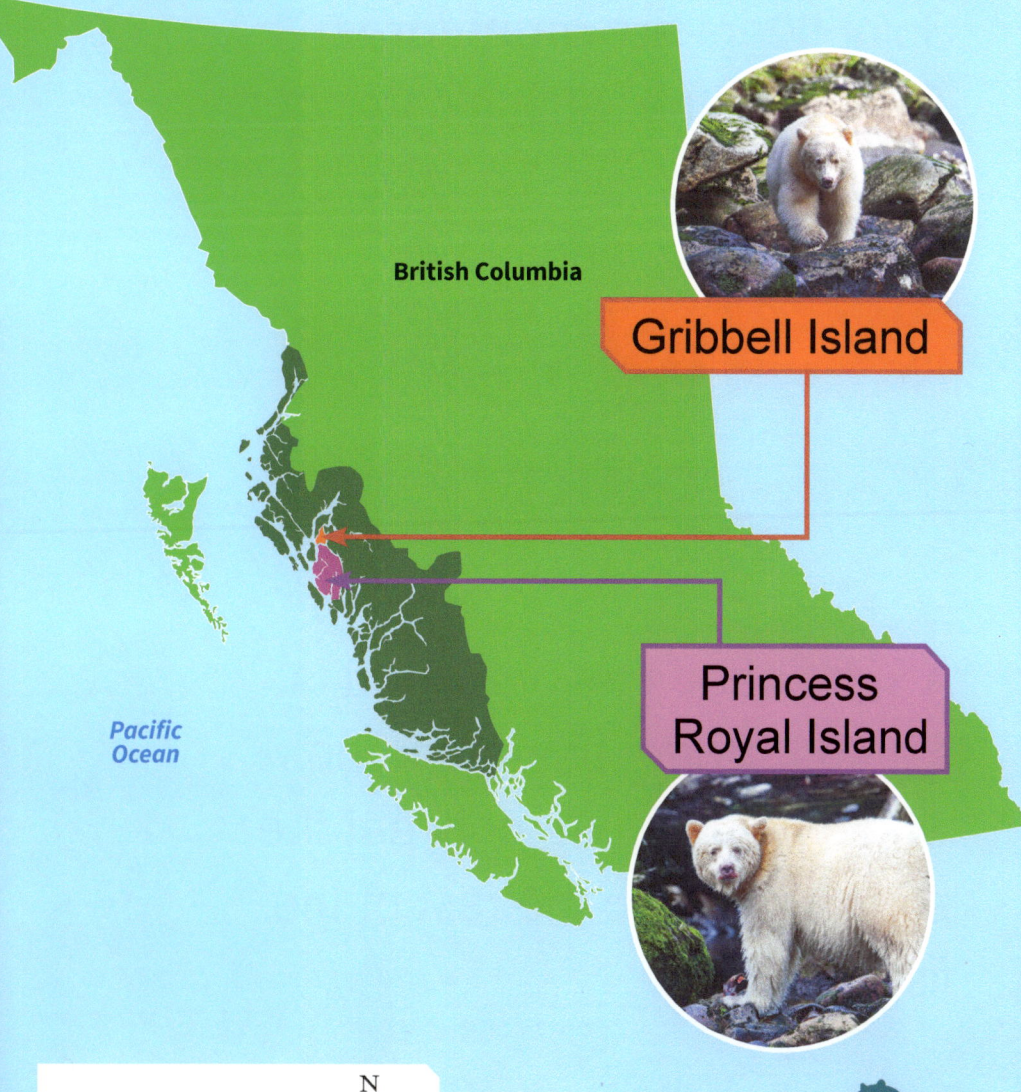

What Do Spirit Bears Eat?

Spirit bears are **omnivores**. They eat other animals like deer, mice, or mussels. They also eat berries, fruits, and grass.

KEY WORD

Omnivores: animals that eat plants as well as other animals.

A spirit bear's favorite food is salmon. Some bears eat the whole fish. Others only eat the eggs and leave the rest of the fish behind.

Spirit bears gain up to 250 pounds (113 kilograms) during the summer.

How Do Spirit Bears Talk to Each Other?

Spirit bears talk to each other by leaving their **scent** on trees for other bears to smell. They do this by rubbing their shoulders, back, and head on the trees. They also use their claws to scratch the trees. This tells other bears where they are.

KEY WORD
Scent: smell.

Bears also use their bodies to show how they feel. Walking away or sitting down can show respect. They may paw the ground or charge if they are scared.

Spirit Bear Life Cycle

Spirit bear babies are called cubs. They are born in their mother's den while she is hibernating. Cubs come out of the den in the spring.

Cubs spend up to a year and a half with their mother. She teaches them how to find food and avoid danger. Then she sends the cubs to live on their own.

Spirit bears are adults at three or four years old. Adults look for another bear to make cubs with. This other bear is called their mate.

Spirit bears can live up to 25 years in the wild. Adult spirit bears do not travel in packs. They live alone for most of their lives.

Curious Facts About Spirit Bears

Spirit bears can stay alive for seven months without food during winter.

Spirit bears can run 34 miles (55 kilometers) per hour.

A spirit bear's sense of smell is 10,000 times better than a human's.

Spirit bears are protected in British Columbia. It is against the law to hunt them.

There are only between 100 and 500 spirit bears in the world.

Spirit bears are better at catching fish than other bears. Fish have a hard time seeing their white fur in the sun.

Where Did Spirit Bears Come From?

Scientists used to think that spirit bears were different from black bears. Now they believe that during the last **Ice Age**, a group of black bears was cut off from other bears. They think this allowed the gene that makes some bears white to be passed down so often.

KEY WORD

Ice Age: a long period of time when Earth is cold and large pieces of ice cover the ground.

Local Indigenous stories say that Raven, or Creator, made every tenth black bear white after the Ice Age. Some say that Raven did this to remind everyone of how hard the Ice Age was. Others say the bears let Raven turn one in ten black bears white. In return, Raven kept them safe during the Ice Age.

How Spirit Bears Help Earth

After catching a salmon, a spirit bear will take it into the forest to eat. Whatever they leave behind when they are done eating gives important ocean **nutrients** to the forest. This helps the forest grow and keeps it healthy.

KEY WORD

Nutrients: something in food that helps people, animals, and plants live and grow.

Earth needs trees to stay healthy. With so few spirit bears left, many people have worked hard to protect the Great Bear Rainforest. This has brought attention to the need to protect other forests.

How Spirit Bears Help Other Animals

Many smaller animals will eat the salmon spirit bears leave in the forest. These include crows, mink, and insects. Some of these animals would not be able to catch a salmon on their own.

If there are too many plant-eating animals in an area, the plants will eventually all be eaten. These animals will then have no food to eat. Spirit bears eat these animals and help make sure there are not too many of them. This helps make sure there is enough food for everyone.

How Spirit Bears Help Humans

Companies like Spirit Bear Lodge offer tours of the Great Bear Rainforest. Many people take these tours hoping to see spirit bears. This has created jobs for a lot of people.

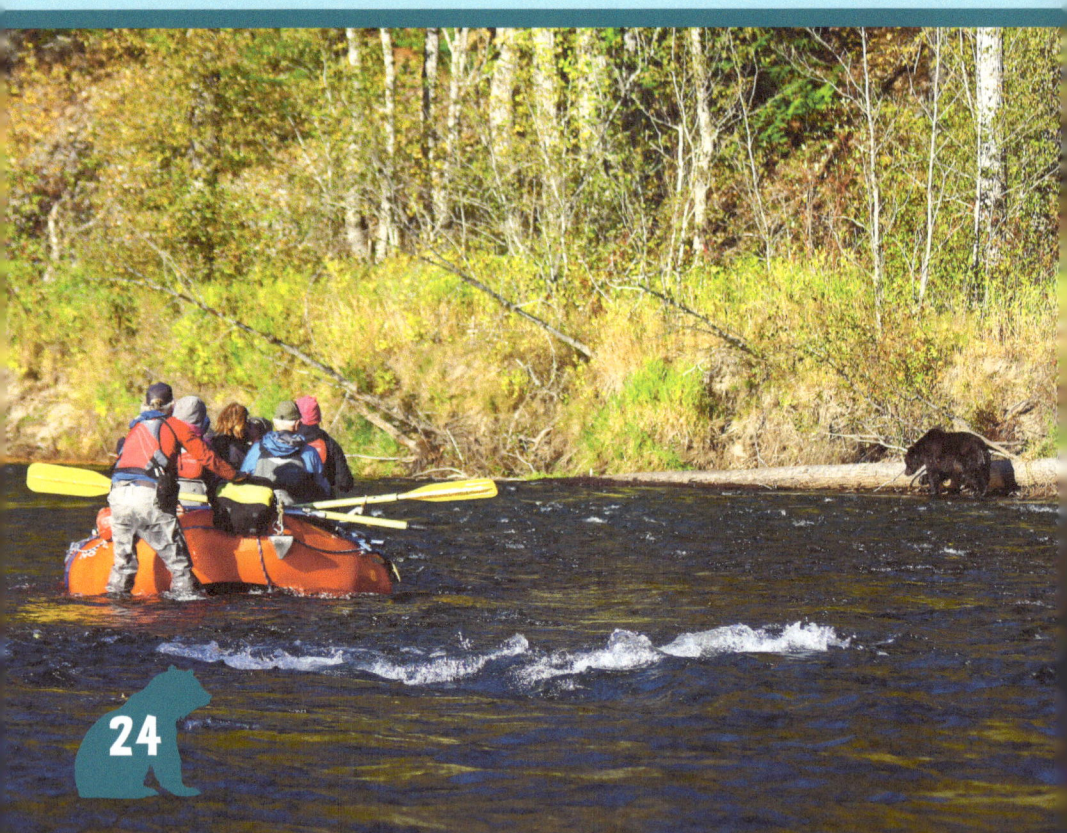

These tours help bring in money for local Indigenous communities. This money goes toward protecting local Indigenous land. Without these tours, the Kitasoo Xai'xais people would not have been able to protect more than half of their land.

Spirit Bears in Danger

It is against the law to hunt spirit bears, but they still face problems. People have fished so much that there are not a lot of wild salmon. This means spirit bears have less food to eat.

Logging makes forests smaller. This means grizzly bears have to move into the forests where spirit bears live. Grizzly bears and spirit bears have to fight for food. Spirit bears often lose.

KEY WORD

Logging: cutting down trees.

How to Help Spirit Bears

The best way to help spirit bears is to learn more about them.
You can visit sites like the North American Bear Center online. Talk with your friends and family. Share all the things you have learned.

Take a tour of the Great Bear Rainforest! The money you pay for the tour will go towards protecting local Indigenous lands. This is also the land spirit bears live on.

Quiz

Test your knowledge of spirit bears by answering the following questions. The questions are based on what you have read in this book. The answers are listed on the bottom of the next page.

1 Who kept spirit bears a secret for many years?

2 What is the name of the forest where most spirit bears live?

3 What is a spirit bear's favorite food?

4 How do spirit bears talk to each other?

5 How long can spirit bears stay alive without food during winter?

6 What kind of bears have to move into the forests where spirit bears live?

Explore other books in the Animals That Make a Difference series

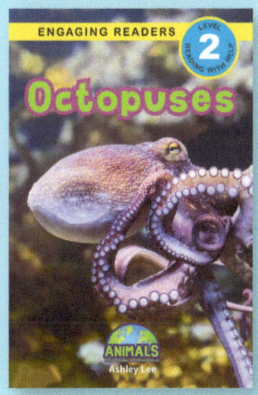
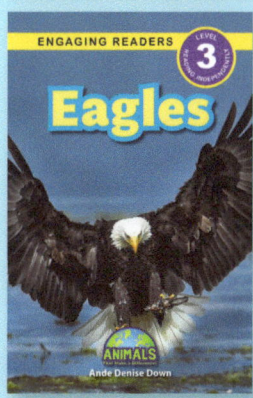

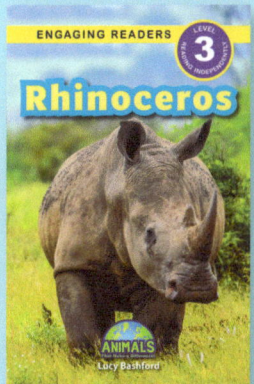

Visit www.engagebooks.com to explore more Engaging Readers.

Answers: 1. Local Indigenous people 2. The Great Bear Rainforest 3. Salmon 4. By leaving their scent on trees for other bears to smell 5. Seven months 6. Grizzly bears

Milton Keynes UK
Ingram Content Group UK Ltd.
UKHW050248081024
449408UK00007B/77